RESPECT ME! RESPECT MY BOUNDARIES!

Empowering kids to set boundaries and to express what's okay and what's not okay

JAYNEEN SANDERS

illustrated by
AMANDA LETCHER

Note to Parents, Caregivers and Educators

While this book may be read in one sitting, I highly recommend revisiting each 'boundary' after the initial read. Take time to explore the concepts and questions together, encouraging meaningful and empowering conversations with your child. Alternatively, you may choose to focus on one 'boundary' per session, allowing space to reflect, discuss and build understanding at your child's pace. There are extensive Discussion Questions on pages 38 to 39 to further draw out the learning.

Note: some children may find it difficult to set a boundary due to shyness or feeling intimidated — and that's okay. What's important is that they know they can always come to you with their concerns. Praise and reassure them for seeking you out. We never want children to feel shame or guilt for not speaking up in the moment. What <u>is</u> essential for children to understand is that they <u>have the right</u> to set boundaries. Practicing boundary-setting and role-playing scenarios at home or in the classroom will help build their confidence.

Jayneen

Respect Me! Respect My Boundaries!
Educate2Empower Publishing an imprint of
UpLoad Publishing Pty Ltd
Victoria Australia
www.upload.com.au

First published in 2026
Text copyright © Jayneen Sanders 2026
Illustration copyright © UpLoad Publishing Pty Ltd 2026

Written by Jayneen Sanders
Illustrations by Amanda Letcher

Jayneen Sanders asserts her right to be identified as the author of this work.
Amanda Letcher asserts her right to be identified as the illustrator of this work.

Designed by Jo Hunt

All rights reserved. No part of this publication may be reproduced, stored in a retrieval system, or transmitted in any way or by any means, electronic, mechanical, photocopying, recording or otherwise, without the prior written permission of UpLoad Publishing Pty Ltd.

ISBN: 9781761160608 (hbk) 9781761160592 (pbk)

 A catalogue record for this book is available from the National Library of Australia

Disclaimer: The information in this book is advice only written by the author based on her advocacy in this area, and her experience working with children as a classroom teacher and mother. The information is not meant to be a substitute for professional advice. If you are concerned about a child's behavior seek professional help.

In this book, you will learn about **SETTING BOUNDARIES** and what to do or say if someone **CROSSES** a boundary you have set.

A boundary is like an invisible fence — we put it in place to keep ourselves safe, both in our feelings and in our bodies.

Boundaries help us to feel **SAFE** and **RESPECTED**.

When we 'set a boundary' we are telling other people **what is okay** and **what is not okay**.

Not everyone will like it when you set a boundary — but that's okay — you are letting a person know **YOUR** rules around **YOUR** body and **YOUR** feelings.

Setting boundaries is not selfish, and it is not unkind. Remember! You have the right to feel **SAFE** and **RESPECTED**, and to **SPEAK UP** if you feel uncomfortable or unsafe.

The boundary setting in this book is **NOT** about things like when to go to bed or cleaning your teeth or eating healthy food.

The boundary setting in **THIS** book is about speaking up boldly for yourself (or another person) when someone is not showing you (or another person) *respect.

> You pushed my little brother off the swing. That is not okay. Jack is feeling sad. You need to be kinder.

*Do you know what '**respect**' means?

Respect means understanding another person's wishes, and caring about them and their wishes. For example, if a person is tickling you and you say 'Stop', that person understands what you have asked for and they stop tickling you straight away.

Boundaries: Body

Everyone has a body boundary — babies, children, teenagers, and adults too!

Your body boundary is the **invisible space** around your body. It's your personal space — a space just for you.

Your body boundary may be invisible, but that doesn't mean it isn't there.

NO ONE should enter your body boundary without your ***consent**.

*What do you think **'consent'** means?

Consent means asking if something is okay or not okay. It means asking for permission. Consent can be shown with words like, 'Yes, I'd like to!' or a very happy 'Yes!' — as long as it is clear that the person saying 'Yes' really wants to be part of it. Consent means everyone feels happy and ready to take part.

People need to ASK for your consent before entering your body boundary.

You have the right to say 'No' or the right to say 'Yes'.

You should NEVER be forced or encouraged into saying 'Yes' to someone entering your body boundary when you really don't want them to.

→ IF YOU CAN'T SAY THE WORDS, WHAT ARE SOME OTHER WAYS YOU CAN SHOW 'NO'?

→ HOW COULD YOU SHOW A HAPPY 'YES' WITHOUT WORDS?

If you DO feel unsafe, you might get a sick tummy or your legs might shake. These are called your Early Warning Signs. There are many Early Warning Signs you can get. You may get one or two, or lots! But if you get any of your Early Warning Signs, please tell a trusted and safe adult on your *Safety Network straight away.

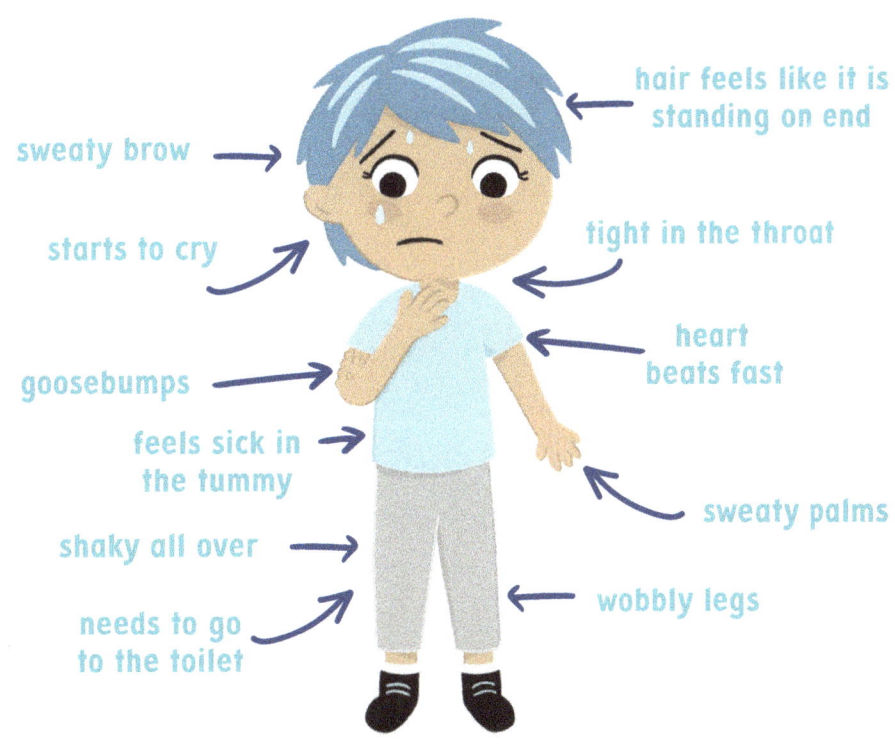

*A **Safety Network** is 3 to 5 safe adults who you trust. These are the people who, if you told them anything that made you feel worried or unsafe, would listen to you, believe you and help you. One adult on your Safety Network should not be in your family.

JUNI'S SAFETY NETWORK

Mama   Dad

Auntie Cass   Ms Janus (teacher)

→ WHAT DO YOU THINK 'TRUST' MEANS?
→ WHO IS ON YOUR SAFETY NETWORK?

People need to ASK for your consent before they enter your body boundary.

And you also need to ASK for a person's consent before you enter their body boundary.

Health workers such as doctors, nurses and dentists need to **ASK** for your consent before entering your body boundary. They need to **ASK** if it's okay or not okay.

One of your safe and trusted adults from your **Safety Network** needs to be with you.

Caregivers, teachers and even family members need to **ASK** for your consent when greeting you or entering your body boundary.

"Can I lift you from your wheelchair?"

"Yes! You can!"

"Remember! If another child, teenager or adult crosses your body boundary and you feel uncomfortable or unsafe, tell a trusted adult from your Safety Network straight away. If they don't help or seem too busy, tell another trusted adult."

"Uncle Davie did not stop tickling me when I said 'Stop!'"

Now we are going to explore some other types of boundaries that include feelings or actions.

HINT! If someone has crossed a boundary, you have the right to tell the person:

1. how they have crossed your boundary.
2. how it made you feel.
3. what you want them to do.

And if they **DON'T** listen to you or stop, you have the right to say clearly:

4. what action you will take.

Boundaries: Time

Sometimes we need to spend time alone or have other things we need to do. We may not want to join in a game or go to a friend's house. **And that's okay!**

You can set a boundary by replying with something kind like:

Hi Lisa! Do you want to come over to my house for a play this afternoon?

Thank you for inviting me, but right now I want to spend some time alone. Maybe I can come over tomorrow — if that's okay for you?

→ **IF YOU NEED TIME ALONE, WHAT MIGHT YOU SAY TO A FRIEND OR FAMILY MEMBER?**

→ **IF A PERSON ASKS YOU TO PLAY AT LUNCHTIME AND YOU WANT TO READ YOUR BOOK INSTEAD, HOW MIGHT YOU SET A BOUNDARY WITH THAT PERSON IN A KIND WAY?**

Boundaries: Private and Public Spaces

PRIVATE means just for you. A private space may be your bedroom or the bathroom. Public spaces, like the kitchen, are shared by everyone.

private space

public space

Sometimes a person may cross a boundary by walking into your bedroom without knocking or asking permission to come in. This is **not okay**. You have the right to say something like:

I don't like it when you come in without knocking. It makes me feel uncomfortable. Next time, I'd like you to knock and wait for my answer before you come into my bedroom.

→ **HAS ANYONE COME INTO YOUR BEDROOM WITHOUT KNOCKING?**

→ **HOW DID YOU FEEL?**

→ **WHAT DID YOU SAY OR DO?**

Boundaries: Photos and Personal Information

People need to **ASK** you before they take your photo or share personal information about you. If they take the time to respect you and ask, you can say it's **okay** or **not okay**. If you are unsure, check in with one of your trusted adults on your Safety Network.

If a person (even an adult) does take your photo or share personal information about you **WITHOUT** asking for your consent, you have the right to say:

You didn't ask me if you could take my photo. I didn't give my consent and that's not okay. I would like you to always ask me before you take my photo or share personal information.

→ HAS ANYONE TAKEN YOUR PHOTO WITHOUT YOUR CONSENT?

→ WHAT DID YOU SAY OR DO?

Boundaries: Not Funny

Sometimes a person may make a joke about a situation, you or another person. The joke may not be respectful, and may hurt your feelings or another person's feelings. A joke like this is **not okay**.

You have the right to set a boundary. You could say something like:

Kenny and I didn't find that funny. What you said hurt Kenny's feelings. I hope that you can be kinder next time.

In this situation, you are not only setting a boundary, you are also being an upstander. An upstander stands up for other people — but only when it is safe to do so.

→ **WHAT MIGHT YOU SAY TO A PERSON IF THEY TOLD AN UNKIND JOKE ABOUT ONE OF YOUR FRIENDS?**

→ **WHY MIGHT IT BE HARD FOR KENNY TO STAND UP FOR HIMSELF?**

→ **WHEN HAVE YOU BEEN AN UPSTANDER? WHAT DID YOU SAY OR DO?**

Boundaries: Unsafe and Unkind Words

Sometimes, another person may say something unsafe or mean and unkind to you or about you. This is **not okay**.

Juni can't play basketball.

You have the right to set a boundary by saying something like:

I don't like how you spoke to me and the things you said about me. Your words hurt my feelings. They made me feel angry and also sad. I would like you to stop speaking unkindly to me and about me.

→ **WHAT MIGHT YOU DO IF THE PERSON DOES NOT SAY THEY ARE SORRY OR IF THEY CONTINUE TO SPEAK UNKINDLY TO YOU?**

→ **WHAT MIGHT YOU DO IF A PERSON SAYS AN UNSAFE THING TO YOU?**

Sometimes, within a group of friends, another person may say something unsafe or mean and unkind about someone in the group or a person in your class or sports team. This is **not okay**.

You have the right to set a boundary by saying something like:

→ **HAS ANYONE SAID SOMETHING UNSAFE OR MEAN AND UNKIND ABOUT SOMEONE ELSE TO YOU? WHAT DID YOU DO?**

→ **WHAT MIGHT YOU DO DIFFERENTLY IF THIS HAPPENS AGAIN?**

Boundaries: Actions that Are Not Respectful

Sometimes, in the playground or at home or at school, a person might:

a) push you

b) speak over you

c) take a toy you are playing with

d) annoy you while you are playing a game.

All of these actions are **not okay**. They are **crossing a boundary**.

Here are some things you could say for each situation.

a) PUSH YOU

1. Pushing me is not okay. You are not showing me respect and you have entered my body boundary without my consent.

2. I feel unsafe.

3. I want you to stop.

4. I will tell Ms Janus if you do it again.

b) SPEAK OVER YOU

1. I don't like it when you speak over me. I have something I want to say.

2. I feel annoyed that you are not showing me respect.

3. I would like you to listen to me and not speak over me.

c) TAKE A TOY YOU ARE PLAYING WITH

1. I was playing with that toy, and you took it from me.

2. I feel sad and also angry that you took my toy.

3. I would like you to give it back to me.

4. You can play with it when I'm finished.

d) ANNOY YOU WHILE YOU ARE PLAYING A GAME

1. You are stopping me from playing my video game.

2. I feel angry when you annoy me like this.

3. I would like you to stop. I would like to play this game by myself.

4. I am going to have to tell Mama if you keep annoying me.

→ HAVE ANY OF THESE THINGS HAPPENED TO YOU? WHAT DID YOU DO?

→ WHAT MIGHT YOU SAY BACK IF THE PERSON SAYS SORRY FOR CROSSING YOUR BOUNDARY?

→ THERE ARE MANY SITUATIONS WHERE BOUNDARIES MAY BE CROSSED. CAN YOU TELL ME ABOUT A TIME SOMEONE CROSSED YOUR BOUNDARY AND WHAT YOU DID? IF IT HAPPENS AGAIN, WHAT MIGHT YOU DO THIS TIME?

Some Things to Remember!

Everybody has different boundaries. What is okay for one person may **NOT** be okay for another person.

When you let a person know they have crossed one of your boundaries, they may not like what you have to say. They may get angry or annoyed. This should not stop you from saying how you feel. However, if at any time you ever feel unsafe, tell a trusted adult on your Safety Network straight away.

You also need to respect other people's boundaries. It's important that you listen to what they have to say with understanding.

Often, it takes courage to let a person know that they have crossed your boundary. But stay strong and speak up if you think a boundary has been crossed.

STOP!

As you grow older, there will be lots of boundaries you will need to set. They may be like the examples we have talked about in this book, or they may be different. Whatever they are, remember you have the right to set boundaries.

→ IF A PERSON ANSWERS YOU BACK IN A GOOD WAY, LIKE, 'I'M SORRY I SPOKE ABOUT YOUR FRIEND LIKE THAT. IT WAS UNKIND OF ME', WHAT MIGHT YOU SAY TO THEM?

You are **NOT** being a 'dibber dobber' or a 'snitch' for standing up for yourself or another person. Setting boundaries is **NOT** about being selfish or unkind. It's about people respecting you and your boundaries.

REMEMBER!

You have the right to feel **SAFE** and **RESPECTED** and to **SPEAK UP** if you feel uncomfortable or unsafe.

Setting Boundaries and Sentence Starters

If someone is crossing your boundary, you may like to tell the person:

1. how they have crossed your boundary.

2. how it made you feel.

3. what you want them to do.

And if they don't listen to you or stop, you have the right to say clearly:

4. what action you will take.

Suggested Sentence Starters

When you ………. I felt ……….
I want you to ……….
If you don't stop ………. I will ……….
I don't like it when you ……….
It makes me feel ……….
I would like you to ……….
What you said makes me feel ……….
If you don't listen to me, I will ……….

Boundary Setting Situations

Here are some situations where you need to set a boundary. What might you say if someone:

- pushed in front of you in the line for the canteen?
- said you had to play a game with them when you really didn't want to?
- asked you for personal information in an online game?
- wanted you to do a project with them when you wanted to do it by yourself?
- showed you unsafe pictures?
- called your friend an unkind name?

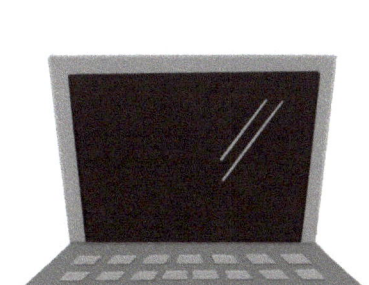

Feeling Words

These words will help you to express how you are feeling if someone crosses your boundary.

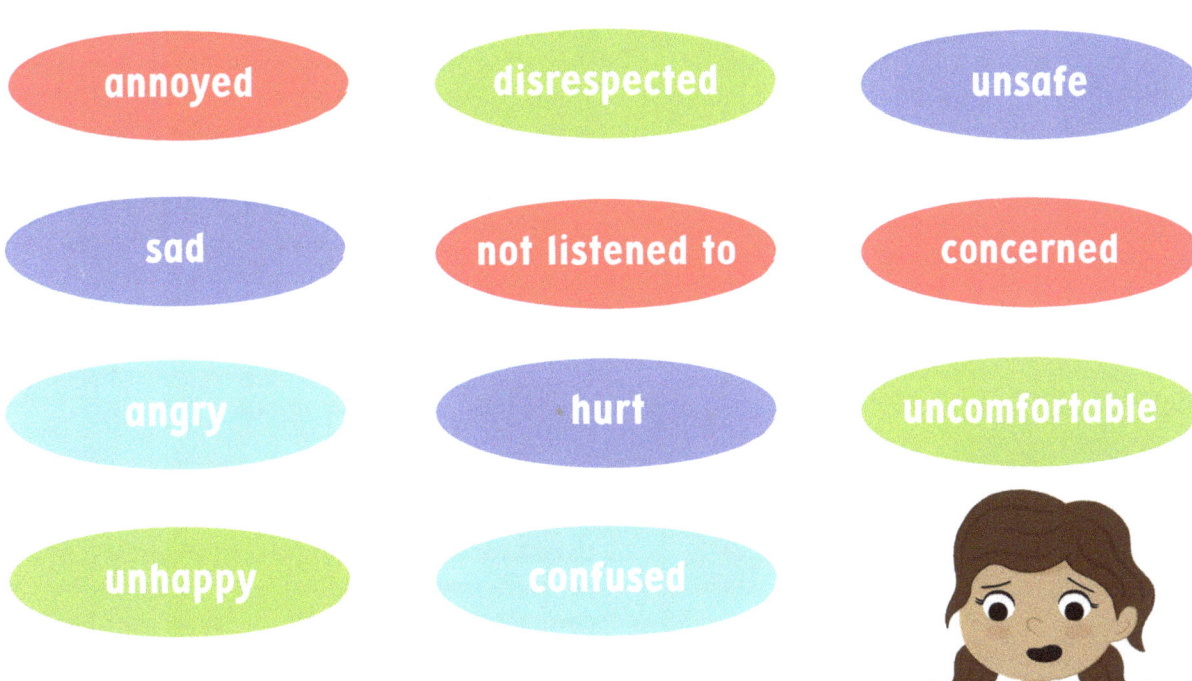

annoyed · disrespected · unsafe

sad · not listened to · concerned

angry · hurt · uncomfortable

unhappy · confused

Discussion Questions for Parents, Caregivers and Educators

The following Discussion Questions are intended as a guide and can be used to initiate an open and empowering dialogue with your child around boundaries, body ownership, consent, respect, feelings and emotions, making choices, recognizing bullying behaviors, and becoming an upstander. The questions are optional and/or can be explored at different readings. Allow your child time to answer the questions both on the internal pages and in this section, as well as encouraging them to ask their own questions around this very important topic. It is equally important that you value their input and listen to their voice. *Note:* if your child feels uncomfortable to speak up when a boundary is being crossed, especially by and older child or adult, be that 'warrior' parent and tell the person how they have crossed your child's boundary. Your child's safety and self-esteem are more important than being polite to someone who is crossing your child's boundaries.

Page 3
Ask, 'What do you think "setting boundaries" means? How might a person cross a boundary you have set?'

Pages 4–5
Ask, 'What do you think "We have the right to" means?' Read each sign and unpack the meaning of each. Ask, 'Do children have the right to feel respected and heard, to speak up and to be safe? Why do you say that?' Encourage your child to stand in a super-hero pose and say each right. Ask, 'Why do you think not everyone will like it when you set a boundary? What rules do you have around your body and your feelings?' Reinforce that setting a boundary, as they will learn in this book, is not selfish and unkind, but is in fact your child's right.

Pages 6–7
Ask, 'Is it okay to ask children to go to bed on time or clean their teeth or eat healthy food? Why do you say that? Do you think the little girl has a right to say that eating healthy foods is crossing her boundary? Why do you say that? What do you think the little girl's grandmother thinks about her setting this boundary? What kind of boundary is Juni setting? Can you give me an example where someone has shown you respect?'

Pages 8–9
Read these pages and answer any questions your child might have around body boundaries and consent. Stand in a super-hero pose with your child and outline your individual body boundaries. Ask, 'Does everyone have a body boundary?'

Pages 10–11
Ask, 'If you didn't want to hug or kiss someone, how might you greet them instead?' *Note:* a high-five, an elbow bump, a wave or blowing a kiss (if they know the person well) are options. Discuss the child's Early Warning Signs on page 11. Ask, 'Have you ever felt any of your Early Warning Signs?' If you child says 'Yes' ask more about when this happened and with whom. With your child, make a Safety Network hand. Using pencil and paper, outline your child's hand, and then write the names of 3 to 5 adults they trust on each digit. These are the people on their Safety Network. Ensure it is always your child's choice who they select for their Safety Network. For more on body safety and consent education, see 'My Body! What I Say Goes!' by Jayneen Sanders.

Pages 12–13
Reinforce to your child that they also need to ask for consent before entering another person's body boundary. Ask, 'Does the doctor or dentist ask for your consent before entering your body boundary?'

Pages 14–15
Reinforce to your child that if they feel unsafe at any time and if someone is not respecting their body boundary, they can come to you or a trusted adult on their Safety Network. Go to the four points on page 15 and discuss. These will become very important as your child learns to set boundaries. Ask, 'Do you remember the four things you can say if someone crosses a boundary you have set?' Have your child repeat them.

Pages 16–17
Ask, 'Is it okay to set a time boundary? Can you give me an example? How might you set a time boundary without hurting someone's feelings?'

Pages 18–19
Ask, 'What does "private" mean? Where are the private spaces in our house? At school? What should people do before entering a private space? What could you say if someone came into the bathroom without knocking first and then not asking permission to come in?'

Pages 20–21
Ask, 'What kind of personal information might be shared? Who would you share this information with? What kind of personal information should not be shared? What should you do if someone asks to take your photo or collect personal information about you and you are feeling unsure or unsafe?'

Pages 22–23
Ask, 'Why is it important to be an upstander? What should you do if you feel unsafe to stand up for a friend?' Say, 'That's right! Move your friend away and tell a trusted adult on your Safety Network about the disrespectful joke.'

Pages 24–27
Note: unfortunately, as younger and younger children have increased access to pornography via screens, some children may be saying unsafe things to others. Ensure your child knows that if someone says an unsafe thing to them or asks them to do an unsafe act, they have the right to say, 'No! This is NOT okay', and to get away as quickly as possible and tell a trusted adult on their Safety Network. Ask, 'Do you have the right to set a boundary when a person is saying mean things to you or about you or about another person in your group? What might you say to them?' Reinforce that it takes courage to set a boundary, but it is very important that they do this. However, if they ever feel unsafe, they need to get away quickly and tell a trusted adult on their Safety Network.

Pages 28–31
Unpack the four scenarios with your child. Revisit and reinforce the four suggested responses from page 15. You could role-play each scenario on pages 29 to 31 and practice how you might each respond using your own words, i.e. stating the action of the offender, how you felt about the offence, what you want the offender to do and what you will do if the offender does not listen to you. You could explore further role-plays using the Boundary Setting Situations on page 37.

Pages 32–35
Unpack each of the Things to Remember on pages 32 and 33. Two general questions might be, 'What do you think this means? Do you have any questions about this cloud and its meaning?' Reinforce that if your child ever feels worried or unsafe about absolutely anything, they can always come to you. Ask, 'What are your rights?'

Pages 36–37
Review these pages with your child. Role-play the Boundary Setting Situations. You and your child might like to use some of the sentence starters and feeling words from these pages.

Books by the Same Author

Body Safety Education
A parents' guide to protecting kids from sexual abuse

This essential and easy-to-read guide contains simple, practical, and age-appropriate ideas on how parents, caregivers and educators can protect children from sexual abuse — ensuring they grow up as assertive and confident teenagers and adults.

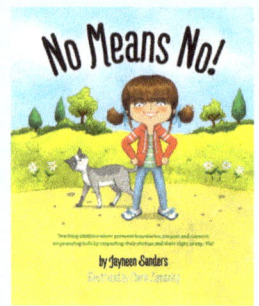

No Means No!

'No Means No!' is a children's picture book about an empowered little girl who has a very strong and clear voice in all issues, especially those relating to her body. This book teaches children about personal boundaries, respect, and consent; empowering kids by respecting their choices and their right to say, 'No!'
Discussion Questions included.
Suitable for children 2 to 9 years.

ABC of Body Safety and Consent

The 26 'key' letters and accompanying words and illustrations will help children to learn and consolidate crucial and life-changing body safety and consent skills.
Discussion Questions included.
Suitable for children 4 to 10 years.

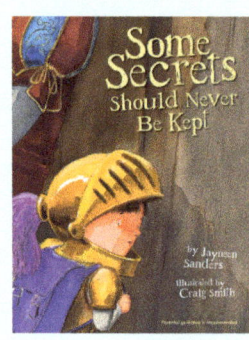

Some Secrets Should Never Be Kept

'Some Secrets Should Never Be Kept' is an award-winning and beautifully illustrated children's book that sensitively raises the subject of inappropriate touch. This book was written as a tool to help parents, caregivers, and teachers broach the subject with children in an age-appropriate and non-threatening way.
Discussion Questions included.
Suitable for children 3 to 11 years.

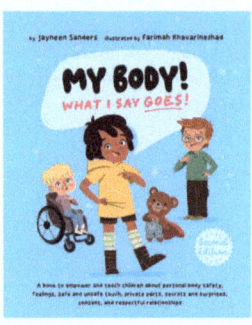

My Body! What I Say Goes!

A children's picture book to empower and teach children about personal body safety, feelings, safe and unsafe touch, private parts, secrets and surprises, consent and respect.
Discussion Questions included.
Suitable for children 3 to 9 years.

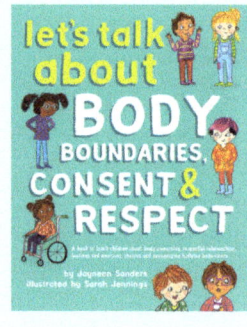

Let's Talk About Body Boundaries, Consent and Respect

Through familiar scenarios, this book opens up crucial conversations with children around consent and respect. A child growing up knowing they have a right to their own personal space, gives that child ownership and choices as to what happens to them. These concepts are presented in a child-friendly and easily-understood manner.
Discussion Questions included.
Suitable for children 4 to 10 years.

My Body Safety Rules

A children's picture book to educate and empower children with disability about body boundaries, consent and body safety skills.
Discussion Questions included.
Suitable for children 5+ years.

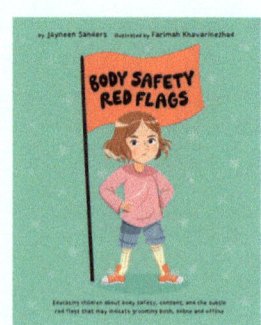

Body Safety Red Flags

Darby will take children, and the adults who care for them, through the subtle 'red flags' that may indicate a child and their family are being groomed. Although a 'tricky' topic, being able to identify grooming red flags is crucial for children and adults to stop abuse before it starts.
Discussion Questions included.
Suitable for children 5 to 11 years.

For more books and free resources go to www.e2epublishing.info

www.ingramcontent.com/pod-product-compliance
Lightning Source LLC
Chambersburg PA
CBHW041427040426
42444CB00022B/3485